desolation : souvenir

Also by Paul Hoover

Poetry
Sonnet 56 (Les Figues, 2009)
Edge and Fold (Apogee Press, 2006)
Poems in Spanish (Omnidawn, 2005)
Winter (Mirror) (Flood Editions, 2002)
Rehearsal in Black (Salt Publications, 2001)
Totem and Shadow: New & Selected Poems (Talisman House, 1999)
Viridian (University of Georgia Press, 1997)
The Novel: A Poem (New Directions, 1990)
Idea (The Figures, 1987)
Nervous Songs (L'Epervier Press, 1986)
Somebody Talks a Lot (The Yellow Press, 1983)
Letter to Einstein Beginning Dear Albert (The Yellow Press, 1979)

Fiction
Saigon, Illinois (Vintage Contemporaries, 1988)

Essays
Fables of Representation (University of Michigan Press, 2004)

Publications Edited
Postmodern American Poetry (W.W. Norton, 2012)
Postmodern American Poetry (W.W. Norton, 1994)
New American Writing, 1986 to present

desolation : souvenir

paul hoover

OMNIDAWN PUBLISHING

RICHMOND, CALIFORNIA

2012

Cover photograph by Tom Waterhouse. "Sometimes They Are a Matter of Patience," 2010. Taken in the Barbican Centre in London. To see other photographs by Tom Waterhouse, visit: http://www.flickr.com/photos/an_untrained_eye

Book cover and interior design by Cassandra Smith

Omnidawn Publishing is committed to preserving ancient forests and natural resources. We elected to print this title on 30% postconsumer recycled paper, processed chlorine-free. As a result, for this printing, we have saved:

2 Trees (40' tall and 6-8" diameter)
945 Gallons of Wastewater
1 million BTUs of Total Energy
60 Pounds of Solid Waste
210 Pounds of Greenhouse Gases

Omnidawn Publishing made this paper choice because our printer, Thomson-Shore, Inc., is a member of Green Press Initiative, a nonprofit program dedicated to supporting authors, publishers, and suppliers in their efforts to reduce their use of fiber obtained from endangered forests.

For more information, visit www.greenpressinitiative.org

Environmental impact estimates were made using the Environmental Defense Paper Calculator. For more information visit: www.edf.org/papercalculator

Library of Congress Cataloging-in-Publication Data

Hoover, Paul, 1946-
Desolation : souvenir / Paul Hoover.
    p. cm.
ISBN 978-1-890650-58-2 (trade pbk. : alk. paper)
I. Title.
PS3558.O6335D47 2012
811'.54--dc23

                    2011051412

Published by Omnidawn Publishing, Richmond, California
www.omnidawn.com   (510) 237-5472   (800) 792-4957
10 9 8 7 6 5 4 3 2 1
ISBN: 978-1-890650-58-2

The works in this volume have appeared in
6 x 6, *Big Bell*, *Caliban*, *Colorado Review*, *Eleksographia*,
Free Poetry, *Interval(le)s*, *Lana Turner*, *Not Enough Night*,
Oráculo (Mexico), *Spillway*, and *Warwick Review*, often
with other titles and in different versions.

CONTENTS

The Windows (The Actual Acts)

desolation : souvenir

infant at the entrance

words are nearly gone
      print falls from voice
voice falls from mind
      noise is never alone
how can you hear a thing
      if there's no mother note

the ancient laws still hold
      our footsteps are man-made
there's a short-cut to the sun
      through a dark wood

a thought so close to life
      it has its pallor
something's quiet in the child
      and something ages
the rest is 'forward dreaming'
      life without the seams

holding us freezing

an icicle in the sun
       is just enough for grace
what can't be seen
       can still be heard
the color of instruction
       is mud between the teeth

something's past knowing
       but not past breaking
the mother image: tree
       our refuge is the future
'you soon feel altogether
       past touching anything'

in a destitute time
       life retires early
the other world endures us
       life is circumstantial

why are children cruel

sublime the double life
      of cash and carry
pain and pleasure
      man is nature's answer
words get in your eyes

sweet suffering world
      please come to evening
your work is so little rewarded
      death is what you need

life makes no preparations
      its presence is enough
to teach us on our knees
      serene evenings pass quickly
not a single chair on fire

another word for earth

hands joined how
      as if in thought dying
as if a song roared
      the rain forgot to pour
what point in space divides us
      which one holds us close

sheerest of walls
      almost transparent
to feel is to fail
      venus envy, filial wail

water and bell
      ringing with each wave
a work of vastness
      too lucid for the mind
behind what wall
      is the private sacrifice

how the white iris feels

at the center of sensation
      which has no edge
the sand mechanic stands
      nothing windswept sleeps

you can't wear a hat
      too far inside your head
after the guillotine
      the impercipient feels
much larger than he is

man is born to die
      the fold holds him well
life is past time
      'words are not the word'
memory's a savant
      shining from its well

the dream and now a field

what is father mooing
       can't quite understand
his promontory mind
       juts well in
he ceases being himself
       or any other man
what's another word for time
       and all our crimes together

vain remedies, nights
       among seen trees
the consolations pour
       those unseen wither
thinking's like a wind
       tying knots in twine
no answer to your question
       nothing need be said

our immortality
       was never guaranteed
the human spoils
       are time and space together
the order of things
       is a number like thirteen
go now and tell the children:
       death misunderstands us

no speaking of this in public

scissors break into knives
    speech breaks into words
a melody for the sheriff
    then a bright marquee
appearances on TV
    are daily more pale

being is an infant
    life's the first encore
for the last thing
    we remember

the word is on parole
    maybe that's why
it remains forever old
    even youth has wrinkles
let it rain its histories
    be what it impales

why they call them *leaves*

death is always taking
      a busman's holiday
alone like a fuse
      I becomes you
finally, it's just me
      a crowd of one gaping

end of the affair
      another snow falls
silence is a pardon
      what has it bequeathed
our time is out of time
      love squandered on the world

we are south of words
      but they are growing tall
mouth sweet, skin cold
      not everything is all
the right time for night glass
      all green men are mortal

thoughts acquire time

ancient egyptian
        suddenly seems so clear
words spent by their allure
        rust on all the gold

seeing alters being
        undying words are few
only two of us
        spoke the language
and we couldn't
        stand each other

the child is absent
        followed in time
by father and mother
        finally no one's there
to know or remember
        why spiders are admired

trees portray the wind

the moment's always wise
      but it dissolves in beer
the crash test dummies
      were wearing high heels
antecedents of the invisible
      to be is what we feel

a living thinking leaf
      scrapes the pavement like a car
from a yellow house
      in a yellow wood
we watch with all our nerves

on my honor, the oil of state
      runs the car of ideation
down the avenue of dreams
      can't think of infinite space
without a footnote present

life was never greener

night is spoken here
      its time is earned and paid
a breathless signal
      white heat
my father as I recall
      always ran east

when death plays
      with a child
it goes out nimble
      comes back cold
life that traitor
      aboard a razor boat

not time but empty rooms
      the sovereign sense regrets
missing the occasion
      it's not that we love nothing
it just hangs around
      seeking a companion

repeat after me

ideas at the brink
     nouns about to sink
a sinister car
     in the land of pleasure
where rain's
     the only measure

small hands in the tomb
     somber shadow, umber meadow
the father says goodbye
     to the child who gave him birth

what will be enough
     when the earth
contains no one
     will the harvest still be full
grass in need of trimming
     the mind of nature canters
all the wind is gone
     no ice, no weather

rend until it is whole

whose life's only instant
       was one of hesitation
standing at the crossroads
       waiting for a sign
ridiculous to think
       eternity really means it

here is your resemblance
       logic is required
to set yourself on fire
       what are the laws of man
from the viewpoint
       of a leopard

something like a goose
       arrives as experience
you are you regardless
       the system is transparent
not space but finally rooms
       the sovereign sense resides in

life is what afflicts us

our pasts are laid out
        we have lived them all
the dead man first
        then the living child

lost satchel at the station
        contains the last message
we're one word past the town
        who named it grand trunk railway
what adds up to an orange
        can you break that down for me

cold ceremonies
        material fears like fires
I couldn't care more
        also the abyss
is behaving carelessly
        the number one's alone
no one to tell it nothing
        no eye to see a thing

how to describe sky blue

to seem also means
       no logic to the senses
life is never as full
       as the season is empty
our deaths are quite near
       also loose-fitting

small and on the verge
       love is just as full
as the season is ready
       the world is disappearing
there's no end to nothing
       an iceberg at a time

last minute confessions
       the end of truth conditions
all the world is hurt
       but its words are sweet to savor
father's cement impressions
       forever on his knees

children pretend to die

that which passes
       collects somewhere
waiting for its meaning
       how's this for a thought
poetry tears the cloth
       even as it repairs it

you don't have to buy it
       to break it
it's a broken season
       too far past *beaucoup*
love's angel is firm
       a beautiful sound, *doloreuse*

mirror rhymes with error
       erde with *mére*
to touch the first land
       you must have swum far
earth's distant as a star
       where all the crimes occur
there are other trees
       beyond the trees we see

the ghost of us is passing

the research has been done
       we can confirm a death
loss of simple breath
       earth's the last message
space is descriptive
       language encrypts it

the father looks
       inside his books
travels far away
       but the children
are always near
       present here forever

the kings have lost their heads
       apollinaire's sun
bleeds at the window
       rends the day to pieces
one actual world
       hysterical as it pleases

after light trespasses

the sun goes in circles
        what is rain saying
most certainly
        something ancient
how modern is that
        nothingness has a name

alarming, the charge
        for lucidity these days
don't call it unity
        but defragmentation
influx of something
        unable to live without us

does the stone ever consider
        what stoniness means
never to be reunited
        with any primal thing
song on the ground
        one leaf on every tree

earth speaks trees

the dead know they are dead
        more than we know we're alive
I write therefore I'm typed
        which is why the children murmur

last and first are badly named
        there is no last world
only first persons
        fate is beauty, madam
of what would be surprising
        some things are unrehearsed

death's too full of being
        immortal of course but filthy
the thump of an iron
        reminds us of the real
the reader stands with back turned
        I, lost in its premonitions

past tense, past time

in what state do we feel
        and where is the border
perhaps the eyes have it
        thinking's only seeing

identical pictures seek difference
        a camera is not the world
lovely wearing a gun
        to the theater and dinner
wearing scotch plaid
        found in the alley dead

dressed in black for breakfast
        each shadow has its statue
no remedy, not today
        what will be has been
the old are always few
        the new ones many

and what is last in us

the child is alarming
     its grave is so clean
what a terror filling it in
     whose father was a gull
whose mother was the sea
     one of the supremes

touch is a form of speech
     close your eyes to imagine
open them to remember
     forms are firm, shapes shift
a box is always a box
     even when collapsed

no such thing as inside a picture
     everything's outside
as history's outside time
     a sculpture's outside granite
but the grain of wood knows
     what shape it really is

yesterday you were here

our time sickness endures
        desire is at its source
we're 'much too far from shore'
        but we've guessed wrong before
thought is an object
        of only one dimension

crimes of the heart
        confetti all over the bed
mother and father
        travel without a map
one twisted, one deviant being
        when love is being made

infinity's only problem
        is the time it has to spend
space it must defend
        it renders unto the dreamer
a lifetime of kneeling
        before the word 'intention'

one size fits all being

mariners who can't swim
       somehow refuse to drown
scratching the water's surface
       fingertips shining
then mind is out of time
       as well we know happens

the youngest god
       is covered with wrinkles
the oldest are smooth-skinned
       who eats his prey eats me

a god has no language
       can't hear us thinking
exists as the space
       between place and map
poetry stands alone
       cellphone on roam
counting down to none
       no one, noon

the present opens empty

you can't play dead for long
        it makes people nervous
and death is so private
        it misses the point entirely
our amusements need us
        onstage and at the wedding

there's a way out of your senses
        underground, to the east
where the emperor's army was buried
        don't crouch in your grave
lie as flat as you can
        so it will know you're there

genie, genius, spirit
        machinic means have struck
a blow you won't survive
        rival hours are passing
no bees in the hive, no hive
        sound returns to its bell

unreality's rare

the absolute if there is one
       the darkest thoughts are trees
with a hint of light behind them
       life has been and is
a miracle death discovers
       in the farthest well-lit room

what had been silent
       staggers back to its voice
consolation roars
       only the sound of life
houses without doors

moral fish and moral laws
       let me sink my teeth in that
now that all is gone
       this thought is on its own
go, my carrion nouns
       seek what you have found

houses without doors

did you ever see
      an owl in flight ever?
but it survives in you
      from something you once read
it's terrible but true
      unreality's rare

the landscape is changed
      by what we think we hear
father will go far
      mother sounds like murder

earth's tune is nearly perfect
      everything is reckless
easy and worth living
      a terrace, a tuba
what an honor, later horror
      is a flower's delicate beauty

sound returns to its bell

identity is double
      beauty's twice the trouble
two eyes in the mirror
      are fearful of the fact
they're equal
      as two egos

moonlight on the ground
      frost on the window
I am now sufficient
      to the absence I imagined
no song can live without it
      the present opens empty

the body is a fool
      too pious, too solemn
a song on accordion
      fate doesn't understand

the count is down to none

no false alarms lately
       time and space are calm
little by little
       trouble becomes us
destination : mirror
       desolation : souvenir

the tomb is unprepared
       for what lies in it
what made the world blink
       for our friend's pleasure

the closer we get to a statue
       the more we're made of plaster
some metaphysical pattern
       is holding up our bones
death is a trick of nature
       one size fits all being
moon, cover our craft
       before we are only breath

crimes of the heart

yesterday you were here
        now, no matter, gone
irony has no meaning
        the taste of me is you

we go to mother earth
        she takes the body in
enfolds it with herself
        applause encore a corpse

even the mode of error
        changes with the fashion
to awaken as an owl
        hear the mice traipsing
every day a little dying
        to wear your being well

whose mother was the sea

the camera opens its eye
        less than a second only
several times tonight
        past-perfect filled the room

in a mist on the fairgrounds
        what is mountain
and what light rain?
        puddles, fists of sky
beaten into the eye
        american vengeance
bison, what's left
        or worth defying

the dead one is enormous
        lying on the couch
much too heavy to move
        larger every day
uncanny scent
        of an over-ripe garden

what will be has been

figures in space
        fall toward no floor
past tense, past time
        what the answers ask

the end of the beginning
        and what is last in us
infants that continue
        toward love and its declensions
age, decline, and death
        or not, as it happens

are we sick enough of the future
        as we pass it every day
there's no signing the rain
        in or out of being

there is no last world

father is language
       mother its meaning
life is a sentence
       death is past time

the parents are aged
       by the death of their child
but his future is secure
       earth speaks trees
each clearing has its thicket
       mind its maze

his death is their pastime
       too short a life to discover
the shadows in a fire
       what future did he imagine
no time even
       to witness a change of fashion

one leaf on every tree

if this can happen
    everything will
we'll miss the gods we were
    shadows cut from sun

after light trespasses
    it stands alone in the room
death's on death's bed
    myth holds a candle
you can feel the end
    breathing through the ceiling

earth draws the final line
    we're knee-deep in language
must travel to infinity
    to see your mother's eyes

present here forever

the song is called an 'air'
      the weight of earth is speaking
the loss of each word massive
      dead flowers, living grave

so poorly loved
      now dearly understood
our friend of the hours lost
      no desert to cross to save you

we were two of you
      & you were time aching
so sweet it's almost suffering
      the ghost of us is passing

earth's distant as a star

we'll fiercely live forever
      we who still remember
the bee inside a flower
      we let the moon run
because it is old
      and half underwater

have faith and you'll eat dove
      in a dark corner of china
its freshly chopped feet
      rolling in the broth
life is all the facts
      at the speed of attention

destiny's souvenirs
      are inexpensively purchased
a pair of stone scissors
      whatever calls out shining
children pretend to die
      come to life again, delighted

no logic to the senses

to speak by touching
        only two of you
can fully comprehend
        the registers of meaning
how to describe sky blue
        with the tips of your fingers

what's the ring tone of snow
        door open to the closed
time is our sickness
        desire is not its cure

what absolute law
        craves and endures us
bows and speaks to a mouse
        one word it understands

our pasts are laid out

a panel of light in the eye
      where someone carries a window
a window is a mirror
      you can see through

there'll be no crying
      in public
stop twisting your face
      like a screw
you're gone from your bed
      and we bleed
from a hundred
      daily incisions

we're born with death in us
      it grows year by year
until life is small
      then not at all
I think therefore I feel
      life is what afflicts us

eternity really means it

grown old together now
      whom could we love better
not infinite pain as the french say
      wet with death's pleasure
but distance that comes so close
      it forces you to touch it

clouds over miami
      and clouds over time
it's always the future somewhere
      we all remember it well
a violent time has great ideas
      peace is full of holes

a thought doesn't happen
      it goes to the brink and returns
unliving is still life
      we have to unlive it again
whatever one loves is
      rend until it is whole

what will be enough

who makes death's bed
       props its head on a pillow
who agrees to die
       there's no child between us
sand in the desert stirring
       where something's still alive

how sweet your mouth tasted
       the first gust of rain
does the rain sleep easy
       death is very tired
repeat after me
       the words that made us live

rain that fell in the milk
       you carried in a pail
memory that won't stand still
       thick honey in the throat
what's hidden in each thing
       and what yawns around us

night is spoken here

one room enters another
      inside the moment, an hour
compounded by ten years
      no way to reach what ends
the present is being dressed
      for what already happened

our ghosts are growing smaller
      but we can feel them breathing
that room is now empty
      life was never greener

the thought of a chair's immortal
      but not the living chair
place it on the sidewalk
      to see how fragile it is
the end before the beginning
      taste of you in a dream

to be is what we feel

what's in your eyes now
        the candle answers
in rhythms of two and three
        the future has no regrets
snow came into focus
        when we were deep in need

meaning as taste and texture
        then as something said
our words are at the ready
        world and time rhyme
when the word's
        too large to see

mother will climb
        farther in the child
the instant chooses us
        what's your secret being
a child has far to go
        trees portray the wind

finally no one's there

all pictures must be true
        but I am dumber struck
by matter's afterglow
        no world has no affairs
unheard words disperse
        no one to take them in

thoughts acquire time
        but they can live without it
where the little foxes go
        to find little foxes
modesty's all the rage
        when it comes to nature

the silence of a noun
        waiting for its engine
I draw you drawing a picture
        photograph your camera
how to recall a history
        without you leaning in it

a crowd of one gaping

or an infant word wanders
    the local highways blind
no one has understood
    the milky world of mind
words age along with us
    they too need repair

thought: the miniseries
    all sequels wait in line
why we call them *leaves*
    remains an intuition

how does night count
    in terms of light years
of the mirror-familiar gods
    which one sees too far
silence is far from reverence
    tragedy asks no questions

let it rain its histories

what's the first cause
        what will last of us
stir of you in the bed
        warmth I can only remember
who will say your name
        who puts his words in you

impossible to bury
        something so alive
a river, living breath
        no speaking of this in public
all time is fictive time
        our pain is on the ceiling

the language of two worlds
        breaks into one together
blood written on the snow
        is a rabbit's or a town's

go now and tell the children

all the lumbering gods
      find it difficult to speak
it's graceless of them to shine
      like furniture in the sun
tidy, well-dressed men
      in limbo, in middle passage

as with doubt, the cloud
      as with the cloud, a mouth
as with a mouth, the mirror
      as with the mirror, light

the dead man reads a book
      on a train between
calcutta and new delhi
      the window shakes like water
a soul is being made
      the dream and now a field

nothing windswept sleeps

you can only see as far
        as the last hesitant star
someone holds you now
        his breath warms your skin
how the white iris feels
        coming up through snow

at the threshold of a forest
        wind has a proposition
it wants us to enter
        bring light into the gloom
the visible is in peril
        it's running out of room

nature's writing a story
        we call it inner distance
you can't look at nothing
        intention takes its picture

ringing with each wave

authority of music
        many times rehearsed
never quite composed
        the rest is not silence
tongues of ash
        bodies of wood

experience and myth
        will pay what they owe
goodbye to all the bees
        an extra yellow chair
leans against the wall
        its shadow also rare

we use the gods for sport
        black horse, black rider
the green man in the grass
        and the history of zero
the actor and the acted
        underfunded, overflowing

sublime the double life

it snows on the laws of perspective
        you can't see through its system
of gridlock and crystal
        from one memory, many pictures
what is a 'texture' of meaning
        why are children cruel

in a café on the pampas
        three rubbles from the river
scraping *boga* onto our plates
        the paraná is a way of being
no piranha there
        only cattle wading

the simpler the sentence
        the more it comes around
we must prepare the child
        for what it already knows
in space, there is no 'where'
        movement alone is home

the mother image: tree

hour most dear, most dire
    not merely the sea
rocking us to sleep
    but the mother of doubt
holding us freezing

to be guilty of a word
    guilty of hope and bone
to stammer in the aisle
    another word for earth

no punishment in love
    only what you deserve
who else might admire
    the depth of your reserve
it's nothing or all the way
    love in our first eyes

words are nearly gone

infant at the entrance
       among us ideal
hears the rain's existence
       survival at both extremes
what will separate
       death and the child

well past painting
       the sun passes out
our son is you and me
       dirt of two lovers
the future's lived now
       being's encore

the song is sad, a vague idea
       the number one's unreal
this is an english mastiff
       the kindest thing in the world

The Windows (The Actual Acts)

"A real armchair leaning against a real window" di Chirico

The world consists of acts.

The actual acts; acts result in worlds.

Whatever is, is actual.

Hypothetical dog chased by a real cat.

Things are possible then they exist.

In what respect is an accident a thing?

Accidents occur when acts go astray.

If an accident occurs in a sentence, is meaning liable?

There's a distant look on possibility's face.

It will never quite exist or become a fact.

Never acting is also an action.

Which do you prefer, the thing or its state?

What objects lack in time, they make up in space.

An object is the actual awaiting further action.

It can wait a long time.

Time is fresh in objects even when they decay.

You can't give one example of time getting old.

Every second, new time is arriving.

Still, some of us are bored.

All that I can imagine is possible for me.

But perhaps not actual.

Possibility is a source of amusement.

Our toys are laid out.

But, all too often, we're unable to act.

Inaction is a waste of possibility.

Action is a waste of impossibility.

Things have hinges; they turn both ways.

Which is why doors are magic.

The priests of the wall.

Why do we say thoughts have direction?

"I was thinking along that line."

A series of thoughts is like a chase scene.

One thought pushes another over some edge.

Time's job is full-time; there's no time off.

Objects serve for a certain period.

Eventually, they fade away.

They were steady workers in the vineyards of space.

You can't imagine something, unless you saw it before.

A pine tree, for instance.

If you never saw a boat, how would you describe it?

Telling is showing.

Seeing something for the first time requires imagination.

You're learning to see how possible it is.

Then it becomes actual.

A manta ray gliding through shallow water.

Frigate birds on a cliff.

Do you see what I'm saying?

It's harder to say what you're seeing.

Possible peach on a possible dish.

A school of possible fish.

Why do we say "temporal object"?

Name one object that exists outside of time.

I once gave the gift of a dozen temporal roses.

Objects famously take up space.

Two lovers struggle in bed for the same space and time.

There is no freedom for objects with names.

They're stuck being themselves.

For example, you can't rename a thing.

It would alter the world too much.

What instead would you call "scissors"?

The red dress has a history.

A world grew up around it, in which the dress was god.

To know an object, you have to know its future.

Many objects were in our mouths as children.

They tasted square or round, hard or soft.

We were seeing with our mouths.

You can't know a thing without knowing its name.

When the name changes, so does the thing.

A new world spreads before it.

All those lost words of agricultural meaning!

The dovecote and the ploughshare.

Don't get your "hackles" up!

Names make everything real.

Even the imaginary.

Nobodaddy. Uncle Sam.

Many objects are private.

They hide in plain sight.

Their private lives, of course, are none of our business.

Objects at the window, gazing out at us.

Impossible objects, never to be seen.

We name a thing when it acts like the thing.

It has its own rhythms and systems.

Some systems are transparent.

Clocks, for instance.

Everyone knows what's going on in there.

Transparency is one of the world's disguises.

We can't know all of anything.

Or even a little of everything.

The mind can manage only one thing at a time.

The beginning, middle, or end.

Can you name a fourth childhood friend?

We are not infinite beings.

Nor are there infinite objects.

Infinity is only a concept, to bring the cosmos near.

But the cosmos doesn't care, and scatters its attentions.

Memory presents one thing at a time.

It wants to linger there, in time and place.

The smell of bread near a bakery.

Wearing your husband's shoes.

There's a thin line between nostalgia and nausea.

The plunge is sharp, the past too shallow.

Possibility is docile.

It's the actual that cares.

If one thing exists, the cosmos isn't empty.

Many things do exist.

Therefore, the cosmos isn't empty.

It just feels empty.

The words we use are strange.

Because they're so familiar.

And states of affairs are constantly passing.

We haven't the time to grieve.

Space is all places, the contained and the container.

Wherever it goes, space is always at home.

It's our local worlds that are distant.

Which is why we carry totems.

Something on a key ring.

Why am I standing here, on this particular road?

What do I represent, the state of my own mind?

The possible is poetic but only feebly so.

Only the impossible leads to great discoveries.

Here's an object of one dimension.

It has no physical nature, because it's a mental object.

Here's an object of two dimensions.

It is called a picture.

Its trees seem almost real.

But we can't go behind them.

Is darkness deeper than light?

They seem to go equally far.

Infinity means: farther than we can see.

What an awesome concept.

But we can think only as far as we can see.

An object always has some degree of thickness.

This sheet of paper, for instance.

Ideas have no dimension, until you write them down.

At the first distraction, they slip out of being.

We have to give them weight.

No idea comes to us completely.

Its second shoe never quite lands.

Ideas can take a thousand years to come into our heads.

They come a long way, down through history.

But they are soon forgotten.

Natural objects are deeply unfamiliar.

Water, rocks, and trees.

They border on the uncanny.

We feel more at home with things we have made.

Sofa on the lawn, flat screen TV.

How do you know the world is round?

Because someone has pictured it for you.

The less fully drawn, the more beautiful the picture.

A single curved line can do the whole job.

Objects contain their own situation.

They're always showing how possible they are.

When an object disappears, its shape remains in place.

An apple, for instance.

Apples look different in French.

They also sound different, when they hit the ground.

To what extent is water an object?

It runs to find its shape.

Then we call it a "body" of water.

What object is eternal?

Even granite wears down.

Fire is not an object.

It's some kind of process, or being.

A picture of the sea is something like the sea.

No picture is perfect, no object either.

Everything is "almost" or "nearly."

Imperfect picture of an imperfect object.

The sea is being as authentic as it can.

But on certain days, the sea is not itself.

That is, not as we had imagined.

A painting's first depiction is of itself.

Therefore, it never departs from reality.

Are curved lines too passionate?

Too personal somehow?

No such thing as two identical pictures.

Breathtaking difference of two silk-screened Warhols.

No such thing as a logical picture.

There are no false pictures.

There are just pictures.

A chair remains true to its image.

Some hint of the chair in a nest of abstract lines.

Because you were thinking chair.

A tree portrays the wind.

Cold air portrays warm breath.

There's evidence everywhere.

When I say mind, you may hear *mined*.

But I know what I'm thinking.

What would be unthinkable?

An object of no shape is unthinkable.

What proof would we have of an imageless world?

No logic to the world, just traditional practice.

Logic is our invention, like haircuts and dating.

First the town, then the sheriff.

How much of my world remains unknown by me?

How much of the language?

The unprocessed world is the cliff edge of perception.

All that is possible is not thinkable.

All that is thinkable is not possible.

The possible suffers the actual.

Then it becomes a fact.

I'm pointed to what I think.

Then I'm alone with my thinking.

Which of my thoughts are yours?

And which are mine alone?

Thoughts have no past or future.

They're always "right now."

Reckless thoughts are the first to be heeded.

Thinking is shaped by speaking.

And writing holds it fast.

The world doesn't care about thinking.

It goes on being the world.

Meanwhile, the future is changing.

Name one thing that remains to be named.

First writing, then speech, then thinking, then perception.

Last of all, the things worth perceiving.

The "shake" of a thought is part of its meaning.

The part that slips past understanding.

Of which we are most fond.

"When" and "what" are of the world.

"If" goes in all directions.

Truth is as close as our senses.

"I could smell him before he arrived."

When you die, your truths go with you.

Wreckage of knowledge, science, mind.

What is meant by an "empty sign"?

We call them empty when they're too full.

"A horse is a horse" is the zenith of thinking.

You can't go any further, as regards the horse.

The horse can go as far as it wishes.

But not beyond its name.

Beauty isn't a matter of strangeness.

It happens when perception deepens the familiar.

The peach is more peach than ever before.

But too much perception can dull even a stone.

What's the "base note" of a mirror?

How deeply it doubles the world?

All, always, infinite, eternal, and never.

Why should we trust these words?

What if I said, "The sky is never dark"?

Would you try to believe me?

Some light is always present.

Stars and distant neon.

That glow from the swamp.

A shrug has meaning in any language.

It passes in silence and says the right thing.

Infinity is smaller than it used to be.

It's down to just an "infinitive series."

Poetry never thinks things through.

It seizes what it needs directly.

Philosophy thinks too much.

But has very little to say.

Poetry never has to say it's sorry.

All it does is sing and gesture.

That's its wisdom.

The wise fool of the arts.

In poetry and music, beauty is in the passing.

Its having been played still resonates in the room.

A word can't be false; it's just doing its job.

Here comes that word, *simpático*, again.

A handsome word in its way.

Simpatia also.

To love such words, do I have to understand them?

A word walks with its candle.

Darkness behind, darkness ahead.

Knowledge faces a dimly lit stage.

It seems that the play is ending.

You can tell from the tone and rhythm.

There are patterns to these things.

An engine flares wildly as it runs out of gas.

We even have to intuit what we know for certain.

What is not murky?

Practical knowledge is not murky.

How to sharpen a knife is transparent to me.

Dull or sharp, a knife couldn't be clearer.

Philosophy, however, requires murky conditions.

That's the whole point.

It's how much smoke you clear.

The philosophy of fire uses metaphors of water.

Can you wrap your mind around that?

While time and space are wrapped around you?

Which is smarter, quartz or stone?

What's the meaning of this sentence?

Philosophy sets no limits on what can be thought.

But personal experience does.

Thought demands a staging place.

Here, there, before, and after.

You can't think your way inside a thing.

You can only think near it.

Thinking is contained by its world.

We are world through and through.

What can be shown has already been said.

What can be shown need not be said.

The told has been shown.

The false is true in its commitment to falseness.

Truth is true in its commitment to truth.

Therefore, truth conditions rule.

No philosophy can proceed without a concept of truth.

Just a little eschatology gets it through the day.

If the many didn't exist, would there still be the one?

Zero is something, and nothing is something.

Contradiction is part of the world's agreement.

But you wouldn't drink black milk.

Or put out a fire with your hair.

We are as close to truth as a painting of the truth.

That is, at a refractory distance.

The limits of my language will have to do.

The *ark* inside *quark*.

That strange word, "enfeebled."

I am what I can glean.

There are thousands of things we've never observed.

A new species of clam being eaten by a new species of bird.

And there's no new man to record it.

To imagine a world is to clean it.

Hard to conceive of a dirty new world.

Our imaginary worlds are aging along with our real ones.

The limits of the world are new every day.

Because the world is shrinking.

Poetry exceeds the limits of language.

The unknown world is happy about that fact.

The syntax of life is birth, life, and death.

Life is the verb.

Some guesses are educated.

But even the educated are guessing.

Poetry works by a zero-sum method.

Equal pressures of emergence and distance.

Attention and movement, turns when there are turns.

Banality is the poetry of no movement at all.

It won't quite die and refuses to give birth.

To model consciousness, you have to draw a picture.

Yeats' intersecting, counter-rotating gyres.

The rhizomes of Jung and Deleuze.

The poetry of chaos has no intersecting lines.

The world falls through.

Metaphor's knot may hold too fast.

In poetry's logic, surprises are required.

Things powerfully don't quite fit.

The rose itself may be of interest.

But poetry is the shadows in its folds.

Anomalies hold little interest.

They sing a note of weary invention.

Not the strange hand but the strangeness of hands.

There are no logical pears.

There are no illogical pears.

They're simply what is given.

Nature used to make all the noise.

Now it makes what we call silence.

A problem in math is stated as a sentence.

There's syntax and grammar.

Its beauty lies in zero.

The dark star of the system.

A tape loop models infinity.

Renewal and boredom to the nth degree.

What's the word for "nth" in German?

Poetry requires a speechless speaker.

Its speaks from a groundless ground.

From the past-future to the future-present.

Its pulse is nothing / song.

Is logic too emotional to be considered math?

They both involve proofs.

But not proofs of existence.

Existence is proof of itself.

You can't go below rain on a stone.

You can't go above it, either.

What we call time is actually fictive time.

We perceive and remember islands of experience.

The rest falls away.

Time is the stage, memory the actor.

Pain results from a certain coherence.

For no visible reason, a person weeps in the street.

Especially, for some reason, in New York City.

Real time is confined to baseball games.

No drama, no coherence.

Experience is whatever interest decides it is.

And that becomes the story.

That business with Charybdis.

Not to mention Calypso and Circe.

Poetry's business is to trade in attention.

Maximum pleasure from maximum pain.

Pain can be funny, when it occurs in others.

Pleasure has the tensile strength and wave rhythm of water.

There's a ripple of thought in the spine.

Pleasure is the final value.

No truth, no pleasure.

By the world, we mean the All.

Where even the vacancies are present.

Nothing less would ever make sense.

Perception lends extra value to the world.

Poetry lends even more.

The tax on it is public inattention.

The world's intentions are pure, because it has none.

But there are certain patterns.

If a buffalo falls through the ice, nothing can save it.

It's impossible to look behind the given.

You're in no position to judge.

But you can speak from behind it, by means of fiction.

A mouse is finally the mouse it started out to be.

Even the mystics would cease their chatter.

Many in silence have no special wisdom.

They simply have nothing to say.

No silence, no song; no noise, no world.

Innocent blood, innocent ax.

The world takes up all the room inside a camera.

A lot more world spills outside the frame.

No world is made of thought alone.

Or music alone or painting.

No thought is made of world alone.

The navigators didn't invent the new land.

They sensed that it was there.

Have you ever gazed from a window to see if everything's still there?

And seen your own face in the glass, superimposed on the view?

Consciousness rests among its objects.

Which makes the objects restless.

It is possible to say, "I no longer recognize the mirror in me."

Or, "The author is the product of the work he produces."

The more illogical it is, the more it's of interest.

Truth is of interest, but it's hard to explain.

You can't locate its beginning or end.

Then the middle goes missing.

Where's the speechless speaker for the unspoken world?

The Bartleby of our day, to stand in the file room dreaming?

When nothing is ordinary, nothing is of interest.

Thought is metaphysical when its motive is distance.

The easy gazers are living in a dream.

The thinker's becoming real.

Is irony too sentimental?

Is its faith in our era waning?

Two new words are needed, "enworlded" and "beselved."

To be enworlded is to be beselved.

To be beside yourself is to be fully conscious.

By the seaside, the beautiful sea.

Is it possible then that I've misunderstood the question?

Paul Hoover is the author of numerous poetry books, including *Sonnet 56, Edge and Fold*, and *Poems in Spanish*, and a collection of literary essays, *Fables of Representation*. He is co-translator of *Beyond the Court Gate: Selected Poems of Nguyen Trai*, the anthology *Black Dog, Black Night: Contemporary Vietnamese Poetry*, and *Selected Poems of Friedrich Hölderlin*, which won the PEN-USA Translation Award. He is also winner of the Frederick Bock Award of *Poetry* and the Jerome J. Shestack Award of *American Poetry Review*. Professor of Creative Writing at San Francisco State University, he is editor of *Postmodern American Poetry: A Norton Anthology*, and co-editor of the literary magazine, *New American Writing*.

desolation : souvenir
by Paul Hoover

Cover text set in Bodoni Std.
Interior text set in Minion Pro.

Cover photograph by Tom Waterhouse. "Sometimes They Are a Matter of
Patience," 2010. Taken in the Barbican Centre in London.
To see other photographs by Tom Waterhouse, visit:
http://www.flickr.com/photos/an_untrained_eye

Cover and interior design by Cassandra Smith

Omnidawn Publishing
Richmond, California
2012

Ken Keegan & Rusty Morrison, Co-Publishers & Senior Editors
Cassandra Smith, Poetry Editor & Book Designer
Gillian Hamel, Poetry Editor & OmniVerse Managing Editor
Sara Mumolo, Poetry Editor & OmniVerse New-Work Editor
Peter Burghardt, Poetry Editor & Bookstore Outreach Manager
Jared Alford, Facebook Editor
Juliana Paslay, Bookstore Outreach & Features Writer
Turner Canty, Features Writer
Craig Santos Perez, Media Consultant